Karate Kata and
Applications 3

By the same authors:
The Karate-do Manual by P. M. V. Morris (Stanley Paul, 1979)
The Advanced Karate Manual (Stanley Paul, 1989)
Karate Kata and Applications 1 (Stanley Paul, 1990)
Karate Kata and Applications 2 (Stanley Paul, 1990)

KARATE KATA

AND APPLICATIONS

3

VINCE MORRIS
&
AIDAN TRIMBLE

STANLEY PAUL

LONDON·SYDNEY·AUCKLAND·JOHANNESBURG

Aidan: To all my past instructors

Vince: To my father, Arnold, who has been more important than perhaps he knows

Stanley Paul & Co. Ltd
An imprint of Random Century Ltd
20 Vauxhall Bridge Road, London SW1V 2SA

Random Century Australia (Pty) Ltd
20 Alfred Street, Milsons Point, Sydney 2061

Random Century New Zealand Limited
PO Box 40-086, Glenfield, Auckland 10

Century Hutchinson South Africa (Pty) Ltd
PO Box 337, Bergvlei 2012, South Africa

First published 1991

© Vince Morris and Aidan Trimble, 1991

Set in 12pt Palatino (Linotron)
Printed and bound in Great Britain by
Butler & Tanner Ltd, Frome and London

British Library Cataloguing in Publication Data
Morris, P. M. V. (P. M. Vincent)
    Karate Katas.
    1. Karate
    I. Title II. Trimble, Aidan
    796.8'153

ISBN 0 09 174588 8

Contents

Acknowledgements

The authors wish to thank the following people for their kindness and helpfulness:

In particular our good friend Keiji Tomiyama, Chief Instructor to Great Britain and Europe for Tani-ha Shito-ryu, for the calligraphy.

Harry Cook for assistance in obtaining the historical photographs.

Chris Hallam and Craig Strong for their help during the photo sequences.

The Sherwood Business and Conference Centre for coffee and room to spread out.

Dominique Shead for calm patience and understanding, plus lunches!

Roddy Bloomfield (well known expert in the art of Real Tennis and erstwhile stunt man) for his enthusiasm for this project.

Kata

Kata are a predetermined series of blocking, evading and countering techniques against single or multiple attackers, who may be armed or unarmed.

In a sense Kata are not peculiar to Eastern fighting arts. That is to say that the concept of providing an instructional manual is not, for these are to be found in many European languages covering arts ranging from medieval swordsmanship to modern-day boxing.

One element stands out, however, as being significantly different in the Oriental Kata. In the majority of cases the Kata are taught to students by example, only rarely were the early techniques recorded in diagrammatic or textual form, on scrolls which were kept secret and passed on only to exceptional students who had proved themselves worthy after many years practice.

Generally these secret scrolls contained brief details of the main instruction which was passed on orally and by example. They were often presented in a deliberately obscure fashion so as to be of little use if they fell into the hands of someone not well versed in the traditions and teachings of that particular school.

Gichin Funakoshi, the 'Father' of modern karate gives a revealing insight into the emphasis placed upon this secrecy.

In his book *Karate-do Nyumon* published in Japan in 1943 (and owing much to his third son Gigo [Yoshitaka] who is to a great extent responsible for the powerful Shotokan karate of today), Funakoshi relates that in the Ryukyu islands the tradition of secrecy was such that no written records were kept. Techniques were passed on by direct instruction from master to student, very often on a one-to-one basis, and the historical background to the Kata was transmitted by oral tradition, a notoriously imprecise method.

He goes on to tell of a communication he received from an elderly Okinawan karate-ka who wished to pass on to him a particular Kata before he died. As Funakoshi himself could not go, he asked that this Kata be taught to Gigo. After instructing Gigo in the

Kata (behind locked doors in a shuttered room) the old man confessed that he had refused to pass on this Kata to anyone before; only once in a crucially altered way to a man who had continually pestered him until he agreed.

Although in most cases the major concern of the scrolls is to catalogue the techniques of the Ryu, a good proportion of the text is given over to the element which distinguishes them from any Western instructional manual; the interweaving of spiritual philosophy with physical violence!

Based on an eclectic Zen Bhuddhist foundation, with intertwining elements of Confucianism and the native Shinto religion, the art of despatching an enemy was raised to a spiritual level.

A group photo showing karate masters Koyu Konishi (second from right), Gichin Funakoshi (far left) and Kenwa Mabuni (seated), 1934. Mabuni was the founder of Shito-ryu

Indeed, so important was this Zen aspect that the same sentiments appear in scrolls of different Ryu, even in those concerned with distinctly different martial arts, such as Archery and Swordsmanship.

To come to a proper understanding of Kata, and to approach a proper practice of Kata it is vital to appreciate how inextricably interwoven is the philosophical element with the purely pragmatic physical side.

Just as this is so in the Kata of the older classical Ryu, so it is in the relatively younger 'schools' of karate, which have been subsumed into the traditional ethos.

Karate can indeed be practised purely as a strong and effective means of fighting. The Okinawan masters developed techniques capable of inflicting severe damage to any attacker and it is quite possible to train solely in the *waza* – the technique of blocking and counterattacking. Even the early practitioners of the art, however, held the spiritual element to be of equal importance to the physical techniques.

The Okinawan fighting arts were not themselves very much under the influence of the mainland Zen ethos, but *Te,* as the indigenous fighting art was known, became naturally subsumed into the martial culture and its Zen ethic upon its importation into Japan.

Even so, before this time there is evidence that certain Okinawan masters (Higaonna and Itosu, to name two) were much concerned that the art of *Te* be taught as a spiritually-orientated discipline.

After studying the history of karate, and indeed of all of the Japanese fighting arts, one has to conclude that it is a mistake to assume that they are inextricably involved with Buddhism, and with Zen in particular. What becomes clear, however, is that any discipline which removes the fear of death and injury, and enables trained reflexes to deal spontaneously and effectively with any threat is much sought after by the warrior.

The experience of the mainland warrior led to the development of a Zen-permeated martial culture, which, as well as imparting through strict discipline and meditation those very sought after qualities, also encouraged the development of individual values which were morally and socially beneficial: a concern for aesthetics and art, poetry and ceremony, belief in the virtues of honesty, dignity and compassion.

Toward the end of the sixteenth century, for example, the Jigenryu martial school, which was essentially concerned with teaching swordsmanship, established a curriculum which as well as concentrating on techniques with sword and dagger also devoted time to practice with spear and bow, and the art of poetry, and the tea ceremony. This was largely due to the influence of the Zen master Zenkicki.

Whether or not many actually attained those qualities which were held to epitomise the 'enlightened' man does not in any way detract from their desirability. The point to reflect upon is that in the original *-jutsu* form or in the later *-do* form a true martial artist is one who has attained mastery of both physical and spiritual aspects.

I have written in greater detail elsewhere *(The Karate-do Manual* and *The Advanced Karate Manual)* of the reasons why this emphasis on the spiritual side came about, but it is of such vital importance to correct understanding and application of Kata that the serious student must be encouraged to learn more of this aspect, and also fully understand that the spirituality – the *Zen* aspect – had a basic pragmatic reason for its emphasis, it made the martial artist a better fighter!

The essence of Zen is a complete acceptance of the inevitability of change; nothing remains the same, the wheel is always turning, leading to the only certainty – at some time or another this human lifespan will come to an end. To place too much importance on this fragile butterfly life was deemed futile; far better to aim at honour and respect, which held society together, even if in pursuance of this it became necessary to give up life. Thus the fighting man defeated his greatest foe – Fear! And specifically the fear of death, which if unconquered could cause that miniscule hesitation in combat that could be fatal.

Hence the importance placed upon gaining 'a mind like water' *(mizu-no-kokoro)* in whose mirror-like surface all actions were reflected and perceived without the ripple of fear to distort the image, allowing the correct response to be made free of all inhibition.

The strict discipline of a continual regime of meditation based upon an acceptance of the transitory nature of all things led the samurai to develop a fearless disregard for the perpetuation of life at all costs, and to foster a strong-willed determination to continue upon a chosen course of action without hesitation, doubt or deflection. Indeed the basis of a formidable fighter!

Anyone, therefore, who wishes to fully understand and gain full benefit from practising the Kata must be prepared to at least con-

Okinawan karate master Motabu showing empi strike

sider carefully that to practise them purely as physical fitness forms or simply as a series of physical techniques is to go against the experience, advice and teaching of some of the most fearless and renowned fighters who ever lived!

There are some fifty Kata practised by the various karate schools today, mostly stemming from the practise and experience of the old masters, and in the Shotokan style we practice some 26 which can be broadly categorised into two groups: those which suit the larger, stronger martial artist, and those which are more appropriate to a lighter, more mobile stature.

The former group, which stress physical strength, were sometimes formally referred to as *Shorei-ryu,* and the latter, which emphasise speed and agility as *Shorin-ryu,* and although the *Shorei-ryu* type are particularly effective for physically conditioning the body it would be wrong to imagine that this was their main function, or that they were practised without the correct mental and spiritual concentration *(Zanshin).*

Likewise, although the two types seem to suit essentially different body types it is a mistake to choose to concentrate solely on the group which, on the surface, would appear most appropriate to your particular build; all the Kata develop a rhythm and co-ordination of movement, and the well-balanced fighter must develop the attributes of both types.

At advanced level it is necessary to select one or two Kata, for in-depth practice, to 'enter deeply' into the soul of the Kata, and at this stage then it would be appropriate to select from the type most suitable to your physical characteristics. Even so the full range of Kata should not be neglected.

The problem

Although the physical practice of the various Kata is in itself an excellent physical exercise, promoting suppleness, flexibility and improved muscle tone, we have seen that this is only part of the story, and that proper practice demands that the martial artist develop *Zanshin* an alert, concentrated awareness of the totality of the situation, with an untroubled 'unstopping' mind allowing complete freedom for appropriate and effective action.

How?

'While performing a Kata, the karate-ka should imagine himself to be surrounded by opponents and be prepared to execute defensive and offensive techniques in any direction.' So urges the late head of the Japan Karate Association, Masatoshi Nakayama, who was himself one of Gichin Funakoshi's students. *(Best Karate,* Kodan-sha International Ltd, 1981.)

This to a student under the direct instruction of a master in a one-to-one learning environment, I suggest, is easier to comply with than is the case with the vast majority of karate-ka practising today. We have seen that much of what is now included within the Kata has been passed on by oral tradition, subject to misperception, misunderstanding and plain forgetfulness, as well as by the deliberate desire to keep the original meanings secret, known only to a trusted few. Even some techniques which, on the face of it, are self-evident, may not be quite what they seem in the Kata, they – like many of the blocks – may be presented in the reverse of the proper direction.

Also we know that many of the Kata practised today have been deliberately altered to make them more suitable for mass transmission, as well as to make them conform to the more athletic nature of present-day techniques and upon occasion to make the practice of them safer. For example, whilst performing the Kata *Chinte* Kanazawa Sensei broke his right hand by striking the back with *Ipponken* causing Master Nakayama to remind him that the Kata should be modified for training purposes. All of which makes the practice of the Kata in line with Nakayama's advice practically impossible, as, in our experience, the vast majority of students have and can only have a rudimentary understanding of the *Bunkai* – the applications of the techniques contained within the Kata.

Takayuki Kubota, Head of Gosoku-ryu Karate in America (The International Karate Association), and well known as an instructor to Law enforcement agencies writes: 'At the moment most people that practise Kata have no idea of its real meaning, or the benefit that it brings. They practise Kata and Kumite as though they were two different things whereas of course Kumite starts with Kata and Kata starts with Kumite.'*

This being so, it is impossible that the Kata be practised fully and completely, and that proper *Zanshin* be exercised.

Yet another problem must be faced. To be practised as was originally intended, that is as a powerful and *effective* means of self-defence, with value in today's society, then it should be obvious that even if all the original *bunkai* were known practice solely related to them would be anachronistic; having little relevance. Sadly, in the world of today attackers are more likely to wield a razor-knife, broken beer-glass or even a gun than a *bo* or *jo*. This latter problem becomes more apparent when one realises that even within the confines of the history of the development of karate techniques the Kata are anachronistic in that they ignore many of the techniques which are widely (and effectively) incorporated into the basic practice of modern karate. Such techniques as: *mawashi-geri* (roundhouse kick), *ushiro-mawashi-geri* (back roundhouse kick), *kakato-geri* (heel or axe kick) and *ushiro-geri* (back kick) are only a few which do not appear in the Kata.

Indeed, this problem exercised the current head of Shotokan Karate International, Hirokazu Kanazawa, to the extent that he began to incorporate *jodan mawashi-geri* into the Kata *Empi*. This move did not find favour, however, and the Kata is currently practised as before, with no roundhouse kick.

It would seem appropriate at some stage for senior *Sensei* to pool ideas and formulate a new Kata, based on the historic principles, but incorporating modern karate techniques.

*Interview with David Chambers in *Fighting Arts* No. 54.

The myth

There is one widespread myth that needs dispelling before we consider the final section of this chapter, the precepts which must be borne in mind when practising the Kata, and that is the racial myth that mastery of karate, and in particular the Kata, is only attainable by the Japanese, for only they can have a real understanding of the martial ethos permeating the art, and can therefore achieve the highest levels of skill.

Frankly this is arrant nonsense!

Let us turn the premise around and hypothesise a native English sport, with philosophical connotations and obscure rules and rituals, deeply rooted in English tradition. Could we then safely assume that no-one but a native-born Englishman would ever excel in the sport, and that no Englishman would ever be beaten by a foreign competitor. Even a cursory glance at the record of the England Cricket team over recent years will serve to underline the ridiculousness of this idea!

Of course there are cogent (financial) reasons for the perpetuation of the myth of Japanese superiority, and indeed there may well be some Japanese who actually believe in it. This does not mean that anyone else need accept it. Indeed, when karate was first introduced to the West, the Japanese were naturally superior, both in skill and understanding, but also in the physical flexibility – especially in the hips and legs – which came to them as a direct consequence of the nature of their society, and which enabled them to have a greater facility in the techniques.

Japanese supremacy has now been challenged, just like the supremacy of English cricketers. At first the Japanese fighters were thought unbeatable, but the records show that the British team has defeated the Japanese on each of the last four occasions when they have fought. The most obvious example is Aidan Trimble's success in Tokyo, the heartland of Japanese karate, when he took on and soundly defeated the best of the world's Shotokan Karate International fighters, including the cream of the Japanese, to become the first World Openweight Kumite Champion.

The point I am going at lengths to make is an important one. If you place any credence in this myth then you set limits to your own progress. There are no limits within the art of karate, only those inherent in each individual practitioner. Believe this and put aside all negative inhibiting ideas.

How to Practise the Kata

As mentioned before, the mental attitude to Kata should be the same as for Kumite. The opponent must actually exist for you, or the Kata will be relegated to the level of mere physical calisthenics. In correct practice it is vital to maintain a sense of urgency and reality, and at every step envisage yourself as actually under threat and attack by a number of assailants determined to do you serious harm.

In this atmosphere *Zanshin* can be developed, and no technique need be 'pulled' short of the target through fear of inflicting damage, as in practice with a partner, and, furthermore, no time can be grabbed for regaining one's breath with these opponents, as they know no rules of fair-play, nor any referee's intervention!

Pragmatically, however, Kata training is a progressive experience which can roughly be defined in three stages.

To begin with, the student has enough to do simply trying to remember the sequence of techniques and changes of direction whilst keeping time to the teacher's count without trying to visualise 'real' opponents.

This is quite in order, for at this stage the technical proficiency and mental awareness are secondary to establishing the pattern of the Kata. Even so, during this process whilst the motor skills and underlying rhythms of the blocking and countering movements are being assimilated, the body is being strengthened, and balance and co-ordination enhanced.

The second stage of development commences when the pattern of the Kata has become firmly established, almost second nature. Now the emphasis is upon specific aims. The student strives to refine his practice, polishing technique and beginning to keep in mind the target areas, the appropriate application of speed and strength, and correct breathing. At this stage, under the direction of an experienced *sensei,* the student is put under increasing physical and mental pressure and begins to become aware of just how important is the power of the mind in physical activity. He or she learns to drag something extra from the depths of the psyche, a strength and stubborness that perhaps has never before been revealed. The body becomes so exhausted from obeying the *sensei*'s command: 'Hai! Now once more!' that it becomes impossible to even keep the eyelids open! Every breath becomes a painful gasp and seemingly must be the last, but even as the body staggers and weakens the spirit shouts: 'I will not give in!' – And from this the lesson is learned that in the depths of your spirit you can never be defeated.

The third stage is properly the practice of 'Moving Zen'. The techniques are by now instinctive and the goal perfection. Practice becomes an intensely private thing, age no longer matters, youthfulness, strength and stamina, even a fully operative body are not prerequisites for this journey. Here the Kata is never for simple display but is a vehicle, a path of absolute determined awareness and concentrated attention.

By this final stage the karate-ka has developed the ability to fuse mind, body and spirit to profound depths. The outward display is secondary to the manifestation of inner power and calm determination. Now the 'stopped' mind is released; fear is defeated by acceptance, and all peripheral anxieties are seen in perspective and set aside as full attention is directed to 'here and now'.

In Karate-do the Kata begin by being concerned with the physical down-to-earths of balance, co-ordination, power, flexibility and so on, but progress to being far, far more.

Each time a Kata is practised (as a whole or in part – by a karate-ka thoroughly familiar with it) it should be a new creation, fresh, dramatic and meaningful in just the same way that a musician recreates a piece that has long featured in his repertoire. It should never be a stale repetition, a bored and boring rendition.

On the contrary, just as the musician 'loses' himself in his music so the karate-ka re-interprets and re-creates the Kata, bringing it to life and imbuing it with his own personality, making each performance the first.

There are occasions, however, when it is beneficial to perform the Kata in different ways. Hirokazu Kanazawa – one of the foremost karate teachers in the world – advocates that every third time it should be performed without power, directing the attention to maintaining *Hara* (concentrating *Ki* below the navel) and at the same time concentrating on the correct tensing and relaxing of the muscles.

An early karate session. Note the students' attire

Many teachers also advocate the practice of Kata in the opposite direction to the normal, thus affording practice on both sides and more deeply ingraining the sequence into the memory.

Aidan and I both strongly advocate that you vary the direction in the *Dojo* in which you regularly practise. This will help ensure that you concentrate wholly on the Kata and the imaginary opponents rather than using a familiar object in your area of vision to help orientate you. Similarly, after taking care to make sure of safety, you should from time to time practise the Kata with your eyes closed.

For the karate-ka interested in Kata competition these last suggestions will be helpful in overcoming the problem of performing in an unfamiliar environment.

In our book *The Advanced Karate Manual* I gave a comprehensive outline of utilising visualisation techniques as an aid to practice. I will simply point out here that this method can prove invaluable in refining the execution and performance of Kata, and is strongly recommended.

A point worth making to the Kata competitor is that the idea of competition is essentially alien to the fundamental concept of Kata, which we have seen to be not for public display but as an aid to the effective execution of Kumite and self-defense. Following this, as Kanazawa comments, the essence lies not in the beauty of movement but in its efficiency.

In many instances today we find that Kata competitors vie with each other to perform the 'flashiest' most acrobatic Kata, complete with side-kicks that go straight up! Thus underlining how far from a proper understanding of their art are both the competitor and the judges who are impressed by external agility rather than internal condition manifested in simple, effective and efficiently executed techniques performed with *Zanshin*.

As a matter of course the *Bunkai* – the application of the techniques – should form part of regular practice with a partner. To make Kata performance meaningful it is necessary to visualise the attackers and their techniques as they would be in reality, and this means constant practice with partners to enable correct judgment of distance and timing.

To begin with the defenses should be the traditional ones which were originally devised to meet each particular attack. Only when thoroughly conversant with these should the *Bunkai* be altered.

If the Kata are not to be relegated to the status of museum pieces, however, it is important that they be applicable to the different circumstances of the modern age, wherein it is most unlikely that an attacker would wield a six-foot *Bo*, but baseball bat, knife, club or gun. Every type of weapon demands a different response in terms of recognising the potential of the weapon and assessing the correct defense. It is a good idea, therefore, to incorporate various weapons into *Bunkai* practice and modify the responsive technique, distance and timing to suit. Of course, by the nature of the Kata, by the secrecy surrounding them, through misunderstanding and by purposeful deception, and by the changes wrought by a variety of masters, it is not always clear just what the original meaning of any particular move was. If this is the case, then we advise consulting the original from which the Shotokan Kata evolved. This will very often provide the clue and help clarify the original purpose. Failing this, it is better to invent your own application than simply to practise the technique as calisthenics. Bear in mind, however, that the application must be efficient and effective, and follow properly from the one preceding and lead without forcing into the one following.

The precepts

The following points should be borne in mind when practising Kata:

Courtesy: karate begins and ends with courtesy, and is signified with the bow *(rei)* at the start and finish. It is important that the state of *zanshin* is apparent in the demeanour from the moment that the karate-ka walks forward to begin the Kata. The stance: heels touching, toes apart, hands lightly touching the thighs *(musubi-dachi)* should be relaxed but alert, the gaze directed straight ahead. A sense of calm determination should be cultivated as the mind and spirit is prepared for the encounters to come *(yoi no kisin)*.

All Kata should begin and end on the same spot on the line of performance *(embusen)*. Proper mastery is not attained until the breathing is harmonised with the execution of technique and posture *(kokyu)*.

Performing any element of the Kata without understanding turns it into an exercise in calisthenics and devalues the practice. You should always bear in mind the application and defend or attack the correct target areas *(tyakugan)* accordingly.

An error that we see quite often is the application of too much force and *kime*. It is important to understand that the Kata contain many movements which do not demand this. Master Funakoshi himself points out: 'The use of strength in continuous, rapid motions does not mean that one is skilled' *(Karate-do Kyohan)*. You must move quickly or slowly as necessary, and only apply strength where appropriate.

Remember that *Yame* at the end of a Kata carries the implication of a continuing state of readiness, so do not 'switch off'. To the true martial artist there is no dividing line between their art and 'real-life'. The art becomes the shaping and refining tool for moulding life, and in turn becomes inextricably an expression of that life. There can be, then, no 'switching off' until life ends.

Pragmatically of course, a state of unawareness has often brought about the sudden end of life!

Key

It is impossible to learn kata only from a book. A good instructor is vital. Diagrams and text should serve as aids to memory. This being so, the direction of movement has been indicated by what should be self-explanatory symbols, which indicate general movement, not necessarily the focus of attention.

NB: All Kata begin and end with the bow of respect *(Rei).*

Chinte

This Kata was renamed *Shoin* by Master Funakoshi, but is now generally known by its former appellation, the Chinese characters of which mean 'strange' or 'unusual hand(s)'. This probably derives from the variety of the distinctive and unusual hand techniques that it contains. These include Middle-knuckle fist *(Naka-daka-ken)*, Two-finger spear-hand *(Nihon-nukite)*, Palm-heel strike *(Teisho)*, Upper elbow strike *(Age-empi-uchi)*, Vertical fist *(Tate-zuki)* and Knife-hand *(Shuto)*. The Chinese origins of the Kata are evident in its use of wide circular movements and the vertical fist punch.

The application of counter-attacks to vital points make this a good Kata to master from a self-defence point of view, even for people of slight stature, as it gives practice in close-range defence which does not rely upon sheer physical strength.

This aspect is frequently overlooked when practising the Kata, and *Karate-ka* often apply too much power and focus in some of the techniques. *Nihon-nukite*, for example, is often thrust forward in a straight line and focused like *Oi-zuki*. More often than not, this will cause the fingers to miss their aim, as too much muscle tension will work against the fine adjustments necessary to ensure accuracy. The correct application is in an upward arc to the target. Practice in the shift from *Fudo-dachi* to *Zenkutsu-dachi* will enable the defender to counter-punch from a stable immobile position with tremendous force.

Chinte

STEP BY STEP

1. Yoi

2.

3. Migi-Tetsui-Uchi

8. Kiba-Dachi
Awase-Shuto-Age-Uke

8a. Front view of fig. 8

9. Turn

9a. Side view of fig. 9

12. Step forward

13. Fudo-Dachi
Tate-Shuto-Uke

14. Zenkutsu-Dachi
Tate-Ken-Gyaku-Zuki

15. Step forward

4. *Bring back fist*

5.

6. *Hidari-Tetsui-Uchi*

7. *Turn*

10. *Fudo-Dachi*
Tate-Shuto-Uke

10a. *Side view of fig. 10*

11. *Zenkutsu-Dachi*
Tate-Ken-Gyaku-Zuki

11a. *Side view of fig. 11*

16. *Fudo-Dachi*
Tate-Shuto-Uke

17. *Zenkutsu-Dachi*
Age-Empi-Uchi Kiai!

KIAI

17a. *Side view of fig. 17*

18. *Turn*

19. Kokutsu-Dachi
Hidari-Chudan-Shuto-Uchi

20. Step forward
Kokutsu-Dachi-Shuto-Uke

21. Jodan-Mae-Geri

22.

27.

27a. Front view of fig. 27

28.

28a. Front view of fig. 28

31.

31a. Front view of fig. 31

32. Kiba-Dachi
Morote-Haito-Barai

32a. Front view of fig. 32

23. Zenkutsu-Dachi
Kosa-Uke

24. Step up Heisoku-
Dachi Naiwan-Sukui-Nage

25.

26. Heisoku-Dachi
Gedan-Tetsui-Uchi

29. Kiba-Dachi
Morote-Haito-Barai

29a. Front view of fig. 29

30. Turn

30a. Front view of fig. 30

33.

33a. Front view of fig. 33

34. Kiba-Dachi
Ryowan-Uchi-Uke

34a. Front view of fig. 34

35. Right leg up

36.

37. Tsuru-Ashi-Dachi
Ryowan-Gamae

38.

42. Gyaku-Ippon-Ken-
Oroshi

43.

44. Zenkutsu-Dachi
Nihon-Nukite-Uchi-Uke

48. Step forward Zenkutsu-Dachi
Nihon-Nukite

49. Right foot in

50. Fudo-Dachi
Chudan-Teisho-Uchi

50a. Front view of fig. 5(

39. *Zenkutsu-Dachi*
Ippon-Ken-Otoshi

40.

41.

45. *Step forward Zenkutsu-Dachi*
Nihon-Nukite

46. *Turn*

47. *Zenkutsu-Dachi*
Nihon-Nukite-Uchi-Uke

51.

51a. *Front view of fig. 51*

52. *Hidari-Teisho-Uchi*

52a. *Front view of fig. 52*

53. Ushiro-Morote-Ippon-Ken

54. Turn

55. Fudo-Dachi Hasami-Uchi Nakadaka-Ippon-Ken. Kiai!

56. Right foot step forward

61. Zenkutsu-Dachi Tate-Ken-Gyaku-Zuki

62. Pull back front foot

63. Heisoku-Dachi Tsutsume-Ken

64. Jump back

57. Fudo-Dachi
Tate-Shuto-Uke

58. Zenkutsu-Dachi
Tate-Ken-Gyaku-Zuki

59. Step forward

60. Fudo-Dachi
Tate-Shuto-Uke

65. Jump back

66. Jump back
Yame

Chinte
APPLICATIONS

a

b

Figs 1-3 *Block the opponent's punch with the forearm then counter with hammerfist strike*

a

b

c

Figs 1-3 *(alternative bunkai) As the opponent grabs your shoulder, make a circular motion with the arm whilst applying an arm lock*

a

b

c

Figs 9-11 *Block the opponent's lunge punch, grasp and punch to the throat*

a

b

c

Figs 15-17 *Block the opponent's lunge punch, grasp the back of his head and pull onto an elbow strike*

d

Figs 20-23 *As you block your opponent with knife-hand block and he grasps your wrist, deliver a front kick to his mid-section. As you land*

Figs 24-25 *Simultaneously block and up-end your opponent as he attacks with a front kick*

Figs 38-42 *As your opponent attacks with lunge punch, in quick succession strike the top of his fist with your right and left one-knuckle fist*

Figs 39-45 *As the opponent grabs your wrist, strike the back of his hand with a left one-knuckle fist. As his grip weakens, disengage and*

back in your stance, break his grasp with your left arm

attack with a finger strike to the eyes

Figs 50-52 *Block the inside of the opponent's lunge punch with palm-heel, and with the opposite hand strike the elbow joint*

Figs 53-55 *As the opponent grabs you from the rear, lift the arms and lean forward to break his grip. Simultaneously strike his*

Figs 50-52 *(alternative bunkai) As the opponent applies a strangle hold, strike to his mid-section with a right and left palm-heel*

mid-section with a left and right one-knuckle fist, turn and strike again

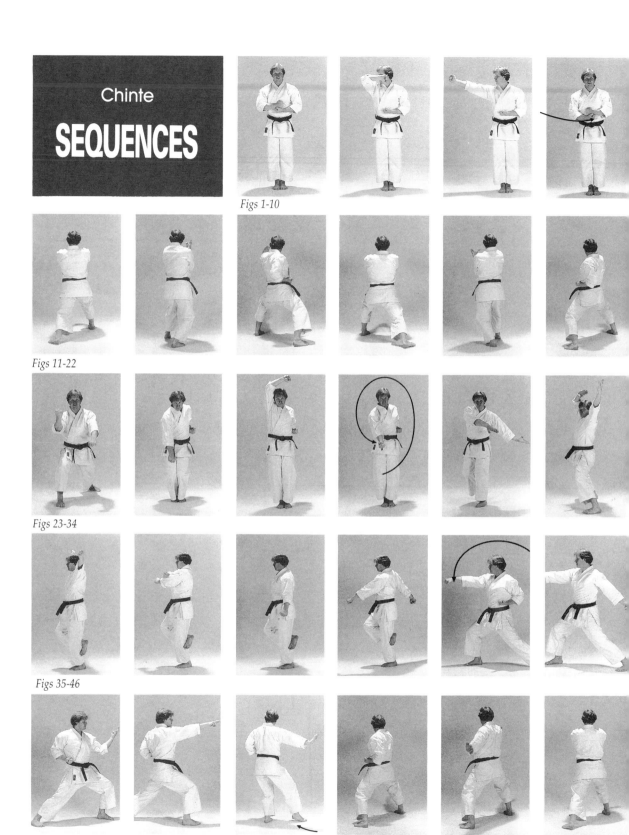

Chinte
SEQUENCES

Figs 1-10

Figs 11-22

Figs 23-34

Figs 35-46

Figs 47-58

Figs 59-66

Unsu

An ancient Kata, apparently of Chinese origin, the name 'cloud hands' signifies that just as the constantly changing movement and nature of clouds is not immediately obvious, so the essence of this Kata – which on the surface is deceptively simple – is in fact a complexity of feints and high and low responses to a variety of attacks. There is also the feeling that the techniques follow powerfully and are as unstoppable and inexorable as the progression of clouds across the sky.

The Kata contains a number of interesting techniques which are often misinterpreted or incorrectly applied, and need some thought before practice, for example the much depicted one-finger attack to the mid-section following the chicken-head block. Few serious *Karate-ka* will even entertain this application, which, against a hard target, would be ineffective and probably cause damage to the finger. Change the area of attack to the eye or larynx, however, following a sweep or unbalancing technique, and the efficacy is revealed.

Again, the traditional reason given for dropping to the floor to avoid and counter a punching attack is not as obvious as would appear. In general it is not a good idea to deliberately go to the ground in any combat situation, but the reasoning here is at least two-fold. The Kata is reminding the student that surprise is often an effective weapon, as is quick thinking where an advantage may be gained in low light levels by perhaps silhouetting an opponent against a lighter background. It is also giving an opportunity to practise defence from a disadvantageous position, where the defender has either been caught in a prone position, or, indeed, has been knocked over. So go beyond the obvious in this Kata and pierce the 'clouds'.

Unsu

STEP
BY
STEP

1. Yoi
Heisoku-Dachi

2.

3.

8. Migi-Ippon-Nukite

9. Keito-Gamae

10.

11. Ashi-Gake

12. Neko-Ashi-Da
Morote-Keito-Uke

17. Keito-Gamae

18. Turn Zenkutsu-Dachi
Tate-Shuto-Uke

19. Gyaku-Zuki

20. Turn

4.

5. *Morote-Seiryuto-Uke*

6. *Step forward*

7. *Neko-Ashi-Dachi Morote-Keito-Uke*

13. *Hidari-Ippon-Nukite*

14. *Keito-Gamae*

15. *Ashi-Gake Neko-Ashi-Dachi Morote-Keito-Uke*

16. *Migi-Ippon-Nukite*

21. *Zenkutsu-Dachi Tate-Shuto-Uke*

22. *Gyaku-Zuki*

23. *Turn*

24. *Zenkutsu-Dachi Tate-Shuto-Uke*

25. Gyaku-Zuki

26. Turn

27. Zenkutsu-Dachi Tate-Shuto-Uke

28. Gyaku-Zuki

29. Drop to floor

34.

35.

36. Migi-Mawashi-Geri

37.

41. Right foot back

41a. Side view of fig. 41

42.

42a. Side view of fig. 42

30.

31.

32. *Hidari-Mawashi-Geri*

33. *Change position*

38. *Feet and hands together*

39.

40. *Kiba-Dachi Morote-Seiryuto-Uke*

40a. *Side view of fig. 40*

43. *Zenkutsu-Dachi Hidari-Keito-Uke Migi-Ushiro-Teisho-Barai*

43a. *Side view of fig. 43*

44. *Left foot back*

45. *Step forward. Zenkutsu-Dachi Migi-Keito-Uke Hidari-Ushiro-Teisho-Barai*

—|— **46.** *Jodan Haito-Uchi*

—|— **47.** *Jodan Mae-Geri*

—|— **47a.** *Side view of fig. 47*

48. *Turn Ippon-Dachi
Jodan Soto-Uke*

—|— **51.** *Migi-Haito-Uchi*

—|— **52.** *Jodan-Mae-Geri*

53. *Turn Ippon-Dachi
Jodan Soto-Uke*

—|— **54.** *Zenkutsu-Dachi
Gyaku-Zuki*

55. *Left foot back
Heisoku-Dachi*

60. *Turn*

—|— **61.** *Zenkutsu-Dachi
Hidari-Gedan-Zuki*

62. *Turn*

63. *Zenkutsu-Dachi
Migi-Gedan-Zuki*

48a. *Side view of fig. 48*

49. *Zenkutsu-Dachi Hidari-Chudan-Gyaku-Zuki*

49a. *Side view of fig. 49*

50. *Turn*

56. *Step 45°*

57. *Migi-Sho-Jodan-Kensei*

58.

59. *Zenkutsu-Dachi Migi-Gedan-Oi-Zuki*

64. *Turn 45°*

65. *Fudo-Dachi Chudan-Tate-Shuto-Uchi*

66.

67. *Zenkutsu-Dachi Teisho-Tate-Hasami- Uchi*

68. Knee up

69. Gedan-Mae-Kekomi Kiai!

70. Zenkutsu-Dachi Hidari-Chudan-Gyaku-Zuki

71. Migi-Chudan-Jun-Zuki

74a. Side view of fig. 74

75. Slide Hidari-Jodan-Haito-Uke

75a. Side view of fig. 75

76. Step through

78a. Side view of fig. 78

79. Slide Migi-Jodan-Haito-Uke

79a. Side view of fig. 79

80. Kiba-Dachi Hidari-Gyaku-Zu

72. *Step through*

73. *Kiba-Dachi Migi-Gedan-Barai*

73a. *Side view of fig. 73*

74. *Turn*

76a. *Side view of fig. 76*

77. *Kiba-Dachi Hidari-Gedan-Barai*

77a. *Side view of fig. 77*

78. *Turn*

80a. *Side view of fig. 80*

81. *Turn*

81a. *Side view of fig. 81*

82. *Kokutsu-Dachi Chudan Haisho-Uke*

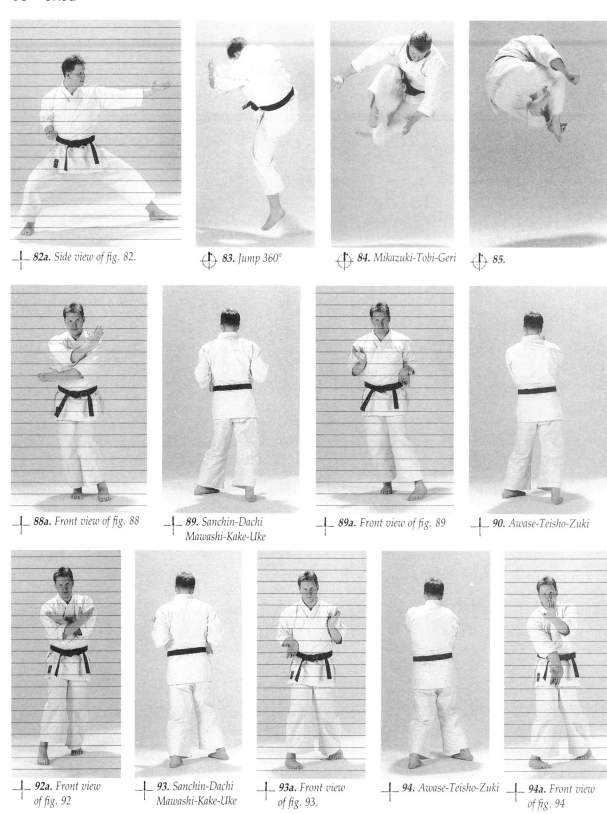

⊥ **82a.** *Side view of fig. 82.*

⊕ **83.** *Jump 360°*

⊕ **84.** *Mikazuki-Tobi-Geri*

⊕ **85.**

⊥ **88a.** *Front view of fig. 88*

⊥ **89.** *Sanchin-Dachi Mawashi-Kake-Uke*

⊥ **89a.** *Front view of fig. 89*

⊥ **90.** *Awase-Teisho-Zuki*

⊥ **92a.** *Front view of fig. 92*

⊥ **93.** *Sanchin-Dachi Mawashi-Kake-Uke*

⊥ **93a.** *Front view of fig. 93.*

⊥ **94.** *Awase-Teisho-Zuki*

⊥ **94a.** *Front view of fig. 94*

_|_ **86.** Ryo-Te-Fuse

_|_ **86a.** Front view of fig. 86

_|_ **87.** Step forward left foot

_|_ **87a.** Front view of fig. 87

_|_ **88.**

_|_ **90a.** Front view of fig. 90

_|_ **91.** Step forward right foot

_|_ **91a.** Front view of fig. 91

_|_ **92.**

95. Turn

_|_ **96.** Zenkutsu-Dachi Jodan-Age-Uke

_|_ **97.** Zenkutsu-Dachi Chudan-Gyaku-Zuki Kiai!

KIAI

_|_ **98.** Yame

Unsu

APPLICATIONS

a

b

Figs 1-5 *Block the opponent's punch with a rising block. Push the opponent's fist across*

a

b

c

d

Figs 1-7 *As the opponent grabs you with both hands, bring your hands inside and up. Wrap around his arms in a circular motion, applying*

a

b

c

Figs 6-9 *Block the opponent's punch with an ox-jaw block, then with the same hand counter with a one-finger strike to the opponent's eye.*

a

b

c

Figs 29-37 *As the opponent sweeps your front leg, drop to the floor whilst delivering a roundhouse kick to the mid-section. Take his front*

d **e**

his body whilst simultaneously attacking with the knee to the mid-section

f **g**

an arm lock. At the same time, step through the opponent's legs, hook his inside leg and take him to the floor

e

At the same time hook his leg, taking him to the floor

e **f**

foot, bringing him to the floor, and finish with a roundhouse kick to the head

Figs 34-36 *As the opponent attacks with roundhouse kick, drop to the floor and deliver roundhouse kick to the stomach or the groin*

Figs 45-47 *Block the opponent's punch with ox-jaw block, then counter with a ridge-hand strike to the head. Continue the attack with a front kick to the throat*

Figs 55-59 *Feint high with the left and right hands as you move forward. As your opponent is distracted, drop low to deliver a punch to the*

Figs 64-71 *Block the opponent's punch, grasp and twist his wrist, and push the elbow upwards with your right hand, applying an arm lock.*

d

groin

d

e

f

Deliver a stamping kick to the hip joint and, as you land forward, deliver a left and right punch to the head and mid-section

(continued overleaf)

g   *h*

a   *b*   *c*

Figs 77-80 *As the opponent grabs your shoulder, raise your arm, twisting your opponent's arm and wrist. Grasp his arm and deliver a close*

b   *c*

Figs 77-80 *(alternative bunkai) Block the opponent's punch with a high block, grasp the arm and counter with a close punch to the mid-section*

punch to the mid-section

Unsu

SEQUENCES

Figs 1-10

Figs 11-22

Figs 23-34

Figs 35-46

Figs 47-58

Figs 59-70

Figs 71-82

Fig 83-94

Figs 95-98

Ji'in

The origin of this Kata is obscure. We know that it was also known as *Shokyo*. There is a belief that the name stems from the Jion Temple, as does *Jion*, and it is often grouped together with *Jion*, *Jutte* and other intermediate Kata.

Some confusion exists over the correct interpretation of the *Kosa-uke* double blocking technique. Logic suggests that the *Gedan-barai* is performed with the same hand as whichever leg is in front, i.e. right *Zenkutsu-dachi/right gedan-barai, left uchi-uke*. This accords with the normal application, the *Uchi-uke* being to synchronize and strengthen *Kime*.

It takes a great deal of practice in order to perform the advancing and turning movements smoothly yet strongly.

Ji'in

STEP BY STEP

1. Yoi

2. Step back

3. Zenkutsu-Dachi Kosa-Uke

8. Step through 45°

9. Zenkutsu-Dachi Hidari-Jodan-Age-Uke

10. Step forward Zenkutsu-Dachi Migi-Chudan-Oi-Zuki

11. Step through 45°

16. Kiba-Dachi Migi-Jodan-Shuto-Uchi

17. Step through

18. Hidari-Jodan-Shuto-Uchi Kiba-Dachi

KIAI

19. Kiba-Dachi Migi-Jodan-Shuto-Uchi Kiai!

20. Turn

4. Step through

5. Kokutsu-Manji-Gamae

6. Turn

7. Kokutsu-Dachi Manji-Gamae

12. Zenkutsu-Dachi Migi-Jodan-Age-Uke

13. Step forward Zenkutsu-Dachi Hidari-Chudan-Oi-Zuki

14. Zenkutsu-Dachi Hidari-Gedan-Barai

15. Step through

21. Zenkutsu-Dachi Kakiwake-Uke

22. Mae-Geri

23. Zenkutsu-Dachi Migi-Chudan-Oi-Zuki

24. Zenkutsu-Dachi Hidari-Chudan-Gyaku-Zuki

25. *Zenkutsu-Dachi Kosa-Uke*

26. *Step 45° Zenkutsu-Dachi Kakiwake-Uke*

27. *Mae-Geri*

28. *Zenkutsu-Dachi Hidari-Chudan-Oi-Zuki*

29. *Zenkutsu-Dachi Migi-Chudan-Gyaku-Zu*

34. *Kiba-Dachi Hidari-Tetsui-Uchi*

35. *Step forward*

36. *Kiba-Dachi Migi-Chudan-Tetsui-Uchi*

37. *Step 45°*

38. *Zenkutsu-Dachi Hidari-Chudan-Tate-Shuto-Uke*

43. *Zenkutsu-Dachi Kosa-Uke*

44. *Turn*

45. *Kiba-Dachi Kosa-Uke*

46. *Kiba-Dachi Morote-Gedan-Uke*

30. Zenkutsu-Dachi Kosa-Uke

31. Turn

32. Kiba-Dachi Migi-Chudan-Tetsui-Uchi

32a. Front view of fig. 32

33. Turn

39. Zenkutsu-Dachi Migi-Chudan-Gyaku-Zuki

40. Zenkutsu-Dachi Hidari-Chudan-Zuki

41. Mae-Geri

42. Step back into Zenkutsu-Dachi Migi-Chudan-Gyaku-Zuki

47. Kiba-Dachi Morote-Chudan-Kosa-Uke

48. Kiba-Dachi Hidari-Jodan-Zuki

49. Kiba-Dachi Migi-Chudan-Zuki Kiai!

KIAI

50. Yame

APPLICATIONS

a   *b*

Figs 1-3 *Block the opponent's kick whilst simultaneously delivering a punch to the jaw*

a   *b*

Figs 15-16 *Block the opponent's punch then attack with a knife-hand strike*

a   *b*   *c*

Figs 30-32 *As the opponent attacks with lunge punch, drop and spin, delivering a hammerfist strike to the mid-section*

d

b

Figs 15-16 (alternative bunkai) *Block the opponent's punch, grasp the punching hand and deliver a knife-hand strike to the elbow joint*

Ji'in
SEQUENCES

Figs 1-10

Figs 11-22

Figs 23-34

Figs 35-46

Figs 47-50

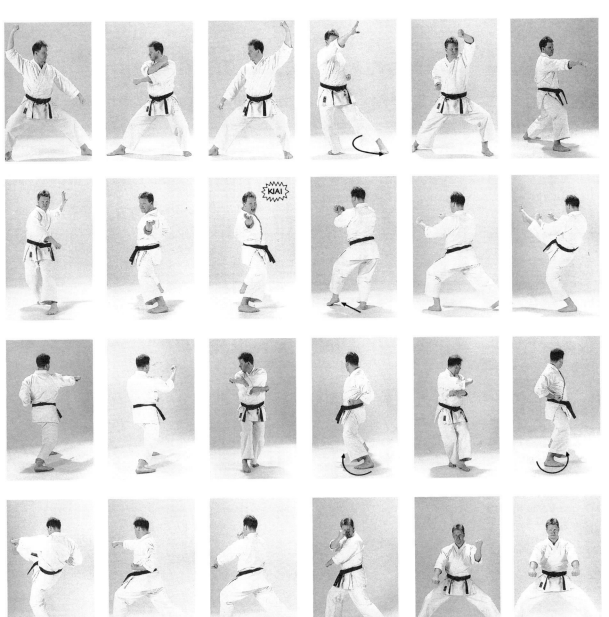

Jutte

This is sometimes transcribed as *Jitte*. The name itself may derive from the distinctive shape formed by the arrangement of the arms in the *Yama-uke* blocking techniques, but is commonly thought to imply that a *Karate-ka* proficient in this Kata has the power of ten men.

A *Shorin-ryu*, *Tomari-te* Kata, *Jutte* incorporates elements of the old *Gyaku-te Waza* grappling techniques, and gives practice in defending against stick attacks.

A fairly short Kata, it should take approximately one minute to perform.

1. Yoi

2.

3. Step backwards

8. Zenkutsu-Dachi
Teisho-Morote-Uke

9. Hidari-Haito-Uke

10. Half-step

11. Kiba-Dachi
Haito-Uchi

17. Kosa-Dachi
Jodan-Juji-Uke

18. Slide left foot
Kiba-Dachi
Ryowan-Gedan-Kakiwake

19. Right foot in

20. Kiba-Dachi
Yama-Kakiwake

21. Turn head

4. *Zenkutsu-Dachi*

5. *Zenkutsu-Dachi Migi-Tekubi-Kake-Uke*

6. *Step 45°*

7.

12. *Left foot in*

13. *Kiba-Dachi Teisho-Uchi*

14. *Step forward Kiba-Dachi Teisho-Uchi*

15. *Step forward Kiba-Dachi Teisho-Uchi*

16. *Right foot in*

22. *Hidari-Mikazuki-Geri*

23. *Kiba-Dachi Yama-Uke*

24. *Migi-Mikazuki-Geri*

25. *Kiba-Dachi Yama-Uke*

26. *Hidari-Mikazuki-Geri*

27. Kiba-Dachi Yama-Uke Kiai!

28. Pull in both feet

29. Shizentai

30. Turn

31. Zenkutsu-Dachi Jodan-Shuto-Uke

34. Sagi-Ashi-Dachi Morote-Bo-Dori

34a. Front view of fig. 34

35. Zenkutsu-Dachi Morote-Bo-Zuki-Dashi

35a. Front view of fig. 35

36. Morote-Koko-Dori

41. Turn

42. Kokutsu-Dachi Manji-Uke

43. Left foot in

44. Zenkutsu-Dachi Hidari-Age-Uke

╆ **31a.** *Front view of fig. 31*

╆ **32.** *Zenkutsu-Dachi Morote-Bo-Uke*

╆ **32a.** *Front view of fig. 32*

╆ **33.** *Morote-Koko-Dori*

╆ **33a.** *Front view of fig. 33*

╆ **37.** *Sagi-Ashi-Dachi Morote-Bo-Dori*

╆ **38.** *Zenkutsu-Dachi Morote-Bo-Zuki-Dashi*

╆ **39.** *Turn*

╆ **40.** *Kokutsu-Dachi Manji-Uke*

╆ **45.** *Step forward. Zenkutsu-Dachi Migi-Age-Uke*

╆ **46.** *Turn*

╆ **47.** *Zenkutsu-Dachi Hidari-Age-Uke*

╆ **48.** *Zenkutsu-Dachi Migi-Age-Uke Kiai!*

KIAI

╆ **49.** *Turn. Yame*

Jutte

APPLICATIONS

a

b

Figs 1-5 *As the opponent attacks with lunge punch, use a downward pressing block and*

a

b

c

Figs 1-5 *(alternative bunkai) Again, block the opponent's punch with a pressing block. This time, twist the wrist and with the left hand*

a

b

c

Figs 9-11 *Block the opponent's punch with an open-hand block, then counter with a ridge-hand strike to the head*

a

b

c

Figs 9-11 *(alternative bunkai) As the opponent grabs your shoulder, grasp his hand whilst making a circular motion with the other arm and*

with the same hand strike with a palm-heel to the jaw

apply an arm lock to the elbow joint

applying an arm lock

a b c

Figs 12-14 *Block the opponent's punch with palm-heel block, grasp the wrist, and step through and strike the elbow joint with palm-heel*

a b c

Figs 12-14 *(alternative bunkai) Block the opponent's punch with palm-heel, step through and strike to the ribs with palm-heel*

a b c

Figs 16-18 *Block bo attack with x-block, pull the bo down and strike opponent with a roundhouse punch to the side of the head*

a b c

Figs 23-25 *Use a high block against the opponent's lunge punch, counter with a crescent kick to the head, and as you land attack with a*

strike, again to the head

a   b   c

Figs 23-24 (*alternative bunkai*) *Use a high block against a bo attack, grasp the bo and counter to the shoulder joint with a crescent kick. With the same leg attack the inside of your opponent's knee with a stamping kick*

a   b   c

Figs 30-35 *Block the opponent's bo attack with knife-hand. On his second attack, grasp the bo with both hands, twist the bo, thus locking his*

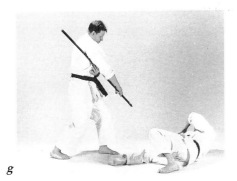

g

e f

arms, and attack with the knee to his mid-section

Jutte

SEQUENCES

Figs 1-10

Figs 11-22

Figs 23-34

Figs 35-46

Figs 47-59

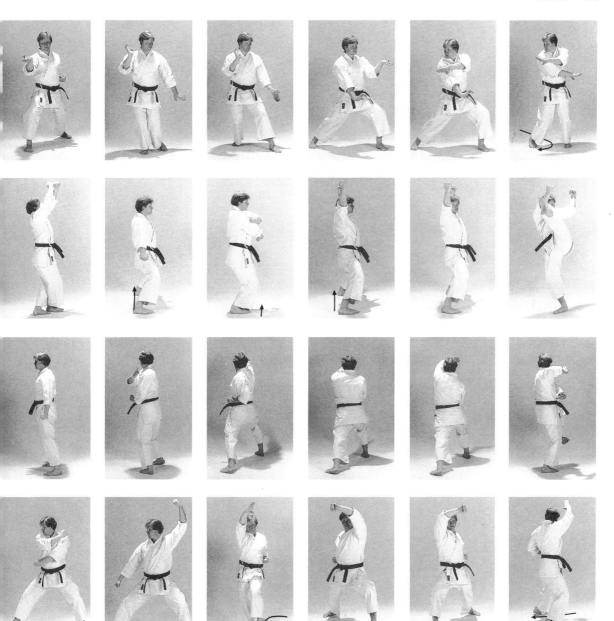

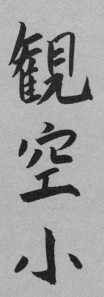

Kanku-sho

This Kata, as explained in *Karate Kata and Applications 2*, derives from *Kanku-Dai* introduced into Okinawa by the Chinese envoy Koshokun. *Kanku-Sho* (the suffix *-Sho*, 'lesser' or 'minor', indicating its origins) was created by Master Yasutsune Itosu.

The basic *embusen* or configuration of the two Kata is very similar in essence, but *Kanku-Sho* devotes most of its attention to middle-level techniques, in contrast to the upper-level bias of *Kanku-dai*. Understanding this should make students aware of such considerations as the difference in height necessary in the two jumping techniques. Often we see height off the ground being made the main criterion in both whereas, although it is a vital factor in the first (to avoid having one's feet swept by *Ashi-barai* or *Bo*), to jump high in the second would be to leap straight into your opponent's attacking technique.

The Kata enables practice in both releasing oneself from wrist grabs and in seizing and pulling an attacker onto a counter. It also offers practice in defending against attackers with sticks and multiple attackers demanding the use of simultaneous blocks with both arms.

In the latter instance, however, it should be pointed out that in this and many other Kata, where double blocks seem evident, it is not always the case. Here, in left back-stance the right fist swings back behind the head in *Jodan Uchi-uke* whilst the left hand simultaneously swings to the front in *Gedan-barai*.

This technique is not necessarily to block an attack to the rear as well as to the front, but, just as with *Jodan Morote-uke* in *Jion*, for example, it is to ensure that both sides of the body are balanced and brought into action together, thus strengthening the *Kime* and, therefore, the effectiveness of the main block.

21. Zenkutsu-Dachi Chudan-Uchi-Uke	**21a.** *Side view of fig. 21*
22. *Chudan-Gyaku-Zuki*	**22a.** *Side view of fig. 22.*

26. *Pull back front foot*

27. *Hidari-Shizentai Gedan-Gamae*

28.

29.

34. *Hidari-Chudan-Osae-Uke*

35. *Kosa-Dachi Migi-Uraken-Uchi*

36. *Step back*

37. *Zenkutsu-Dachi Chudan-Uchi-Uke*

38. *Zenkutsu-Dachi Chudan-Gyaku-Zuki*

39. *Jun-Zuki*

40. *Turn*

41. *Kokutsu-Dachi Migi-Ken-Yoko Uchi-Uke Hidari-Ken-Gedan-Barai*

45a. *Front view of fig. 45*

46. *Slide*

46a. *Front view of fig. 46.*

48a. *Front view of fig. 48*

49. *Kokutsu-Dachi Manji-Uke*

49a. *Front view of fig. 49*

42. Pull back front foot

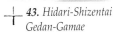
43. Hidari-Shizentai
Gedan-Gamae

44. Turn

45. Kokutsu-Dachi
Manji-Uke

47. Kiba-Dachi
Morote-Zuki

47a. Front view of fig. 47

48. Turn

50. Slide

50a. Front view of fig. 50

51. Kiba-Dachi
Morote-Zuki

51a. *Front view of fig. 51*

52. *Pull right foot in*

52a. *Front view of fig. 52*

53. *Step forward*

55a. *Front view of fig. 55*

56. *Jump*

57. *Turn*

58. *Kokutsu-Dachi*
Migi-Shuto-Uke

63.

64. *Yoko-Keage*
Uraken-Doji-Uchi

65. *Zenkutsu-Dachi*
Hidari-Mae-Empi

66. *Turn*

__ **53a.** *Front view of fig. 53*

__|__ **54.** *Kokutsu-Dachi Bo-Uke*

__|__ **54a.** *Front view of fig. 54*

__|__ **55.** *Slide forward Kokutsu-Dachi Bo-Dori-Zuki-Otoshi*

__ **59.**

__|__ **60.** *Yoko-Kaege Uraken-Doji-Uchi*

__|__ **61.** *Zenkutsu-Dachi Migi-Mae-Empi*

__|__ **62.** *Pull right foot in*

__ **67.** *Zenkutsu-Dachi*

__|__ **68.**

__|__ **69.** *Soete-Kake-Dori*

__|__ **70.** *Tsukami-Dori Migi-Mae-Geri*

┴ **71.** *Hidari-Chudan Osae-Uke*

┴ **72.** *Kosa-Dachi Migi-Uraken-Uchi*

┼ **73.** *Step back*

┴ **74.** *Zenkutsu-Dachi Chudan-Uchi-Uke*

┴ **79.** *Jodan-Haishu-Uke*

⊕ **80.**

⊕ **81.** *Jodan-Tobi-Mikazuki-Geri*

⊕ **82.**

┼ **88.** *Step forward Kokutsu-Dachi Chudan-Shuto-Uke*

⊕ **89.** *Turn*

┼ **90.** *Zenkutsu-Dachi Hidari-Uchi-Uke*

┼ **91.** *Step forward Zenkutsu-Dachi Migi-Oi-Zuki*

75. *Chudan-Gyaku-Zuki*

76. *Chudan-Jun-Zuki*

77. *Lean forwards*

78.

83.

84. *Ryote-Fuse*

85. *Jump and change stance*

86.

87. *Kokutsu-Dachi Morote-Gedan-Shuto-Uke*

92. *Turn*

93. *Zenkutsu-Dachi Migi-Chudan-Uchi-Uke*

94. *Step forward Zenkutsu-Dachi Hidari-Oi-Zuki. Kiai!*

KIAI

95. *Yame*

Kanku-Sho
APPLICATIONS

a *b*

Figs 9-11 *As the opponent grasps your arm, pull your arm into a block position,*

a *b* *c*

Figs 14-19 *Block the opponent's punch with a circular knife-hand block and grasp the hand. At the same time attack with a front kick to the*

a

Fig 25 *As the opponent attacks with a lunge punch, simultaneously block and counter with hammerfist to the groin*

a *b* *c*

Figs 52-55 *As the opponent attacks with a bo, block grasp and twist it with both hands, unbalancing your opponent. Force him to the floor*

d

twisting your opponent's wrist. Attack with a lunge punch to the head

e

f

jaw then back fist to the face

b

c

Figs 25-27 *Block the opponent's front kick as he lands forward. Move the weight forward and strike to the groin with a close punch while covering with the left hand*

e

f

and, using the bo, attack to the mid-section

Figs 56-58 *As the opponent attacks with a bo strike to the legs, jump and spin 360°. As you land, block his second attack, grasp the bo, step*

Figs 62-65 *Block the opponent's reverse punch whilst simultaneously countering with a snap kick to the groin. Grasp the back of his head*

Figs 77-84 *Block the opponent's bo attack, then with one continuous movement strike the bo with a crescent kick, creating an opening. Spin back kick to the mid-section or groin*

Figs 77-88 *Block the opponent's lunge punch, jump and spin, delivering a crescent kick to the head. As you land, drop low to avoid the Step forward with knife-hand strike to the head*

forward and counter with knife-hand strike

and pull onto a roundhouse elbow strike

and drop to the floor, simultaneously delivering a

second opponent's attack. As he continues his attack with a front kick, switch your stance, keeping low, and block with knife hand.

Kanku-Sho

SEQUENCES

Figs 1-10

Figs 11-22

Figs 23-34

Figs 35-46

Figs 47-58

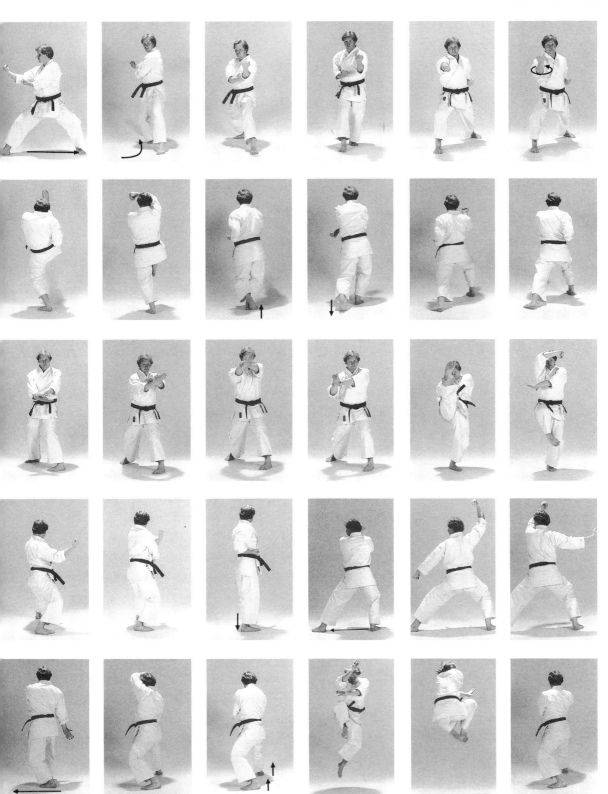

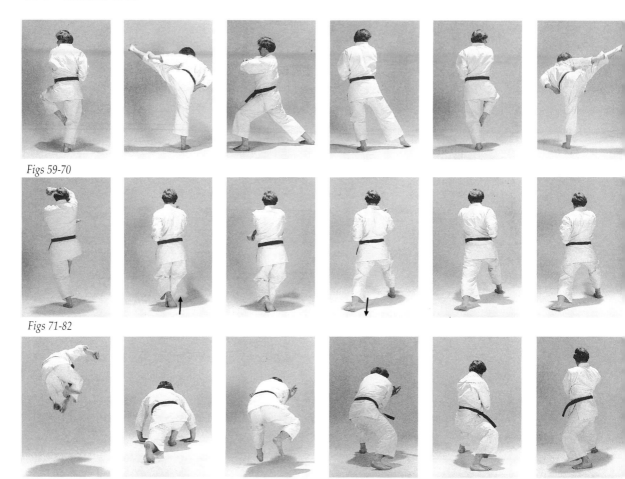

Figs 59-70

Figs 71-82

Figs 83-94

Figs 95

五十四歩小

Gojushiho-Sho

As previously mentioned, the Federation of Shotokan Karate follows the practice of designating the Kata containing the one-finger techniques as '-sho', and the Kata utilising the four-finger techniques as '-dai'.

Many interesting techniques appear in this Kata which bear study. Not the least being the *Keito-nagashi-uke* into *Ippon-nukite*, and the remarks concerning the use of *Ippon-nukite* in *Unsu* should be referred to. Although one-finger strikes to the body are possible for a *Karate-ka* with especially conditioned hands, in general practice the *bunkai* should include applications against soft-tissue targets, or should substitute the one-finger strike with a less inherently dangerous technique.

This Kata also features *Haito* as a blocking technique against punches, kicks or *Bo* attack; *Hira-shihon-nukite* to the groin, and the unusual *Washide* (Eagle-hand) strike.

Gojushiho-Sho

STEP BY STEP

⊥ *1.* Yoi

⊥ *2.* Step forward

⊥ *3.* Zenkutsu-Dachi
Uraken-Gamae

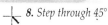

⊥ *8.* Step through 45°

⊥ *9.* Zenkutsu-Dachi
Chudan-Tate-Shuto-Uke

⊥ *10.* Chudan-Gyaku-Zuki

⊥ *11.* Jun-Zuki

⊥ *16.* Chudan-Gyaku-Zuki

⊥ *17.* Jun-Zuki

⊥ *18.* Mae-Geri

⊥ *19.* Zenkutsu-Dachi
Gyaku-Zuki

4. Step through 45°

5. *Zenkutsu-Dachi Heiko-Tate-Zuki*

6. *Step through 45°*

7. *Zenkutsu-Dachi Heiko-Tate-Zuki*

12. *Mae-Geri*

13. *Zenkutsu-Dachi Chudan-Gyaku-Zuki*

14. *Step through 45°*

15. *Zenkutsu-Dachi Tate-Shuto-Uke*

20. *Step right foot*

21. *Zenkutsu-Dachi Jodan-Age-Empi*

22. *Turn*

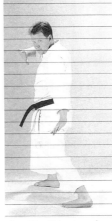

22a. *Side view of fig. 22*

23. *Zenkutsu-Dachi Koko-Hiza-Kuzushi*

23a. Front view of fig. 23

24. Step forward Nekoashi-Dachi Migi-Keito-Uke

24a. Front view of fig. 24

25. Migi-Keito-Nagashi-Uke Hidari-Gedan-Shuto-Osae

25a. Front view of fig. 25

28a. Front view of fig. 28

29. Turn Nekoashi-Dachi Migi-Gedan-Haito-Uke

30. Migi-Keito-Uke

31. Migi-Keito-Nagashi-Uke Hidari-Gedan-Shuto-Osae

32. Migi-Ippon Nukite

37. Step over into Kosa-Dachi

38. Jodan-Koko-Morote-Uke

39. Kiba-Dachi Sukumen Gedan-Morote-Uke

40. Kiba-Dachi-Morote Kaishu-Gedan-Uke

26. *Slide Nekoashi-Dachi Migi-Ippon-Nukite*

26a. *Front view of fig. 26*

27. *Hidari-Ippon-Nukite*

27a. *Front view of fig. 27*

28. *Migi-Ippon-Nukite*

33. *Hidari-Ippon-Nukite*

34. *Migi-Ippon-Nukite*

35. *Turn*

36. *Kiba-Dachi-Morote Kaishu-Gedan-Uke*

41. *Step over Kosa-Dachi*

42. *Jodan-Koko-Morote-Uke*

43. *Kiba-Dachi Sokumen Gedan-Morote-Uke*

44. *Nekoashi-Dachi Migi-Keito-Uke*

45. *Nekoashi-Dachi Migi-Keito-Uke Nagashi-Hidari-Gedan-Shuto-Osae*

46. *Slide. Nekoashi-Dachi Migi-Ippon-Nukite*

47. *Hidari-Ippon-Nukite*

48. *Migi-Ippon-Nukite*

49. *Turn*

55. *Zenkutsu-Dachi Hidari-Uraken-Uchi*

56. *Step forward*

57. *Zenkutsu-Dachi Washite-Otoshi-Uchi*

58. *Zenkutsu-Dachi Washite-Age-Uchi*

59. *Mae-Geri*

63. *Migi-Keito-Uke*

64. *Migi-Keito-Nagashi-Uke Hidari-Gedan-Shuto-Osae*

65. *Migi-Ippon-Nukite*

66. *Hidari-Ippon-Nukite*

67. *Migi-Ippon-Nukite*

50. *Zenkutsu-Dachi Migi-Gedan-Shuto-Uchi* | **51.** *Step forward* | **52.** *Zenkutsu-Dachi Migi-Uraken-Uchi* | **53.** *Zenkutsu-Dachi Hidari-Gedan-Shuto-Uchi* | **54.** *Step forward*

60. *Gedan-Kosa-Zuki* | **61.** *Zenkutsu-Dachi Hidari-Jodan-Empi-Uchi Ushiro-Gedan-Barai* | **61a.** *Side view of fig. 61* | **62.** *Step up Nekoashi-Dachi*

68. *Turn* | **69.** *Kiba-Dachi-Morote Kaishu-Gedan-Uke* | **70.** *Step over Kosa-Dachi* | **71.** *Ippon-Dachi-Chudan Tate-Shuto-Uke*

72. *Kiba-Dachi Tate-Shihon-Nukite Yoko-Hari-Empi*

73. *Turn*

74. *Kiba-Dachi-Morote Kaishu-Gedan-Uke*

79. *Step forward*

80. *Zenkutsu-Dachi Jodan-Uraken-Gamae*

81. *Step back. Hidari-Chudan-Tetsui-Uchi Kiba-Dachi*

82. *Step forward. Migi-Chudan-Oi-Zuki Zenkutsu-Dachi. Kiai!*

83. *Shizentai-Suihe Hiji-Gamae*

88. *Nekoashi-Dachi-Morote Gedan-Shuto-Nagashi-Uke*

89. *Nekoashi-Dachi Morote-Keito-Uke*

89a. *Front view of fig. 89*

90. *Slide. Nekoashi-Dachi Morote-Chudan-Ippon-Nukite. Kiai!*

75. Step over
Kosa-Dachi

76. Ippon-Dachi

77. Ippon-Dachi-Chudan
Tate-Shuto-Uke

78. Kiba-Dachi Tate-
Shihon-Nukite Hari-Empi

84. Shizentai Ushiro-
Tetsui-Hasami-Uchi

85. Shizentai-Suihei
Hiji-Gamae

86. Zenkutsu-Dachi
Suihei-Hiji-Uchi

87. Step forward
Nekoashi-Dachi

90a. Front view of
fig. 90

91. Turn. Migi-Gedan-
Haito-Uke Nekoashi-
Dachi

92. Nekoashi-Dachi
Migi-Keito-Uke

93. Yame

Gojushiho-Sho

APPLICATIONS

a

b

Figs 22-23 *As the opponent attacks with front kick, hook the kick with the left hand, then here your opponent can be forced to the floor*

a

b

c

Figs 23-26 *As the opponent grabs your wrist, turn and twist the wrist whilst simultaneously pushing the left hand through in a pressing Attack with one-finger strike to the throat*

a

b

c

Figs 25-26 *Block the opponent's lunge punch with an ox-jaw block, then block his reverse punch with a downward block, whilst countering with a one-finger strike to the opponent's throat*

a

b

c

Figs 38-39 *Block the opponent's bo attack, grasp the bo and push the bo across his body, unbalancing him and bringing him to the floor*

apply a lock with the right hand. From

motion breaking your opponent's grip.

Figs 70-72 Block the opponent's punch, grasp his arm and attack with straight-finger strike to the throat

Figs 88-90 Block the opponent's front kick with downward block, then block his reverse punch with an ox-jaw block. As you counter with one-

e

finger strike to the throat, simultaneously hook the inside leg and take the opponent to the floor

Gojushiho-Sho
SEQUENCES

Figs 1-10

Figs 11-22

Figs 23-34

Figs 35-46

Figs 47-58

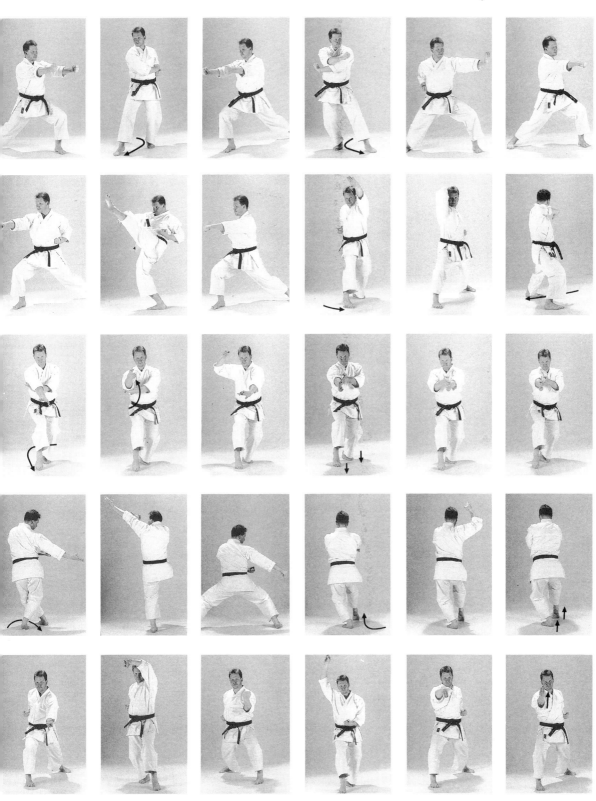

Figs 59-70

Figs 71-82

Figs 83-93

APPENDIX

For those who would like to read further on some of the subjects dealt with in this book, we recommend the following magazines:

Magazines

American Karate, Ed. David Weiss, 351 West 54th Street, New York, NY 10019, USA.

Combat, Ed. Bey Logan, 135 Aldridge Road, Perry Barr, Birmingham B42 2ET.

Fighting Arts International, Ed. Terry O'Neill, PO Box 26, Birkenhead, Merseyside L43 4YQ.

Martial Arts Illustrated, Ed. Bob Sykes, Revenue Chambers, St Peters Street, Huddersfield HD1 1DL.

Shotokan Karate Magazine, Ed. John Cheetham, 1 Grove Court, Lymm, Cheshire.

Traditional Karate, Ed. Bey Logan, 135 Aldridge Road, Perry Barr, Birmingham B42 2ET.

Useful Addresses

The Federation of Shotokan Karate, PO Box 47, West PDO, Nottingham NG8 2EA.

The National Coaching Foundation, 4 College Close, Beckett Park, Leeds LS6 3QH.

Errata

Unfortunately some errors crept into Books 1 and 2 at printing stage. These will be corrected in future editions.

Book 1
Heian Shodan Applications: the caption for Figs 11-13 should read hammerfist strike

Heian Shodan Step By Step: the caption for fig 13 should read Tetsui-Uchi

Heian Sandan Step By Step: fig 51 should have a 'kiai'

Bassai-Dai Step By Step: the following four photos should be inserted between figs 46 and 47:

Book 2
Hangetsu Step By Step: fig 28 should not have an arrow or a 'kiai'